#5

HAMPTONS

BY
~~LUCAS HUNT~~

NEW YORK
THANE & PROSE
2019

"Whenever you feel like criticizing any one," he told me, "just remember that all the people in this world haven't had the advantages that you've had."

—The Great Gatsby by F. Scott Fitzgerald

To Cole and Cael

CONTENTS

ANNOUNCEMENT

First came forsythia
and quick-flowering dogwood
then ornamental cherry tree
with yellow-green buds.

MEMORIAL DAY

The question of what to wear
is always there. Evening
begins like every other day.
A savage ache for leisure.

Let's offend the usual thing.
A car down wooded lane,
mansions of green and white.
The sun sings in waves.

Oysters on silver trays
iced buckets of Champagne.
Tradition is alive. A few
died or committed suicide.

The season brings new faces.
High on a patio, lips curl
for the first of many
pictures of summer people.

LONG ISLAND

Shells, vacuous Atlantic, decompose
under shadow–laden cells of sky,
seaweed corona, yellow waste
and salty wreckage strung
with evidence tomorrow's no sure day—
drab carapace, orb burning out,
blue amplitudes over dunes
cremate bones, enrapt twilight,
nebulous fingers off remote firefields,
submarine shapes birth volumes,
wild parades combine decades
of solitary growth with common clay,
empty bowls crown the earth, gold departs.

DUNES

From a porch on narrow dunes,
a shell to appreciate the flood and fall,
birds sing invisible tremolos
to the vanishing point.

Airplanes and boats rumble on bay,
vehicles cross the bridge
and a sun pours porcelain fire
through cloudless sky.

Insular place, affluent people
come fresh off expressway and train,
where sea foam runs
in sandy fields of jeweled light.

STEAK NIGHT AT THE SHACK

You may wonder why we are here to remember,
Gather round to watch the pallets burn,
    men just off work
Drinking beer in plastic lawn chairs,
Smoking cigars and talking about fish piled
    on a boat at sea.

A distant dog barks as Murphy explains how
    the butcher cut the meat
Thick and true, pound for pound
It's prime beef, he says,
We are men and will eat like men.

But before potatoes are sliced and seasoned,
Before romaine, mushrooms, tomatoes, peppers
    get thrown together,
Before shrimp cocktail, horseradish sauce
    and hot garlic bread,
Before the cork pops—
Games commence, horseshoes and darts
    with a simple system of bets,
Classic rock blasts from the driveway,
    songs of love that is new
As the sunset glows amid leafless trees.

>—→

To fishermen and electricians
    who share their catch with friends
and string the yard with lights
    so our games can go all night.

There have been parties here.
The police were called, no one was hurt.
Now the fire is ten feet high, summer returns
And aromas of dinner drift out the kitchen.

One at a time we head inside to wash our hands
    and crack new cans of beer,
Clear, wipe then set the table
With bowls of pilaf, creamy spinach,
And sautéed onions to pile on empty plates.

Finally, without ceremony,
The large glass platter of steaming steaks arrives
    fresh from the grill,
Mel forks one out to each of us then sits down,
No one says grace yet the cost of life
    has been implied—
We are men and will eat like men.

Nothing is more beautiful than a moment,
sunny scene full of easy dreams of future physical love,
water reflects the trees in joyous silence,
vehicles roll by at dangerous speed
    yet are not there,
        just distraction,
a helicopter's wind-whipping noise shifts
    as grasshoppers rub aloud,
the blue sky is not sad nor stillness burdensome,
    time passes closer than it ever has before,
the music of memory serenades a sitter
        not din, interference or cacophony.

BAY WINDOW

Rainwater drips off rhododendron,
leaves droop, buds upright,
pitch pines and black oaks sway
like a child's first dance.

FOR JAMES

The news came a peaceful spring morning
birds at play, grass in the green
a freshly mown Friday.
Pull on the door
from within
you will not appear
again in the physical world.
I remember your laugh
on a long day,
worker of wood,
thoughts danced in your heart
without having to speak.
Thank you for a job
when there were none and a home
when there was nowhere to go.
You know the flight of spirits in space
the secret trajectory of grace
surpasses information;
all that you gave
returns each moment, now you are forever.

Truth is not fixed for all to see
but a bird, worm in mouth,
lands on fence, leaves.

Broken light falls on
wood beams shorn to fit,
and gets pieced together again.

Horses graze on grass,
hooves stomp on the earth
in rhythm, small clouds ascend.

FLOWER SHOP

It's a madness, a fever, a response
to the question, why end?
The heavy heat of prolonged
day circulates, vines
twist in air. Something
radiant shimmers in stoplight
and sprinkler spray,
ducks and dogs
pace a fenced-in yard
immune to the restaurant,
free from traffic
and evening cartoons
of fancy crowds that fade—
shadows on a fence
flowers in the window
I watch her walk
in dim streetlight.
Then car doors swallow
her and through
a crucial, empty spot—
sunflowers, white carnations
in vases on a long shelf,
the flower shop closed, its lights on.

THE PHILOSOPHER

He said we were not living life fully
and was right, sipping wine so
casually as my schedule
fell apart, survival
and the social contract
dissolved. "No one cares what
you do with your life—
live purposefully before it's too late."

POOL PARTY

A fly-like bee pollinates
small purple flowers
called crocus.
You light
the water on fire
with a piano serenade
eyes guns of joy
paella wet
vodka clean
then surface topless
from the deep.
The water
touches everything
at once,
others play chicken
while we kiss.

Fresh trout from the market, white wine for the host,
everything changes, women in the kitchen
articulate in dresses
saucers sparkle on a silver platter
let's toast—a vibration
the architect wants an answer—
summon words and send
without passion
the end. Why compromise a dream?
Take the meaning to heart
return to friends
gathered at the table
for food, flowers and smiles from above
let's toast—lips like full purses
inhale a cigarette,
say we have met before
then what water does to the earth, over and over.

Does love change you
can't change
summer people
here for the season
water and wind
sun on skin.

I don't care if you say
pink is the blue sky
planes going out come in.

What miracles
we bike a sandy lane
reach the end
without falling down
at the dirt road
Jeff plays our song—
I've been sleeping for too long
hibernating from your love…

Montauk sunrise over
the stink of shellfish
harbor seagulls
ride above

>——>

the Surf Lodge
sunset lovers
saw Leon Bridges
sing *baby, baby, baby*
I'm coming home
clouds sway
like horseshoes
and things get away.

We cross Main Street
for juice and beer
back door
gravel alley
motel parking lot
worn dirt path
in the grass
bodies bent in waves—
drunk crying girls
supposedly
a happy place
beach blankets
by the Sloppy Tuna,
rainbow kites and
lifeguards high on stands,

➤—→

little balls paddled
back and forth
to casual conversation,
dancing on sand
songs become
the story of our moment.

Easter Island motels line
the shore like totems,
a pool to rinse off
Beach House
for cold drinks
barely wearing clothes
looking for
boots, bracelets
from Latin America
then a sunset at Montauket.

The sun just went behind
mountainous clouds
it's the start
of a new night life
we shower
cut the collar
off a dress shirt

>⟶

make it a strap collar
would you prefer
tequila, vodka, whiskey?

Let's take hits
the car will be here
in five minutes
to Ruschmeyer's—
pencil on the pavement
sea above a ball field
beer can driveway
arrow sign past
tombstone benches
concrete fountain
grass cracked asphalt,
someone did donuts
in the parking lot again.

Trees move
a bicycle does not
stars replace fish
your arms
a marble tomb
the language of love

➤——→

below waves
all that's left
of summer
is one dreamsong
or another,
a patient breeze
caressing leafless trees,
glorious flag
outside the club
time to go in again.

Love is life
is love now—
let's do it all tomorrow.

TREASURE ISLAND

A journey in the night alters things
for good. Today is new
because we reached the limits
of grassy wetland,
watery marsh.
Property lines do not
exist in the dark.
Ghosts fly
around a barn,
smoke cigarettes on porch steps.
Trees have eyes—
backyard to moonlit sea
beyond this paradise
floats a land just out of reach.

WATCHING HORSES;
FOR MARY FRENCH

Lovers call from the green
wild and transcendent
(no limit, summer)
flared dresses
dance from tents,
bright polos are bulls
to the bar for free
bourbon and Champagne,
life casually passes,
we nose the air
for fragrant perfume
a new way—
horses trot to field
in gallant display
of leg over leg,
coats a ribbed finery,
sable coursers
lunge with calm fury
as I dream
of waves and toast
the field aglow,
let's hit
a poolside benefit
then after party
before summer fades away.

INDEPENDENCE

Hamburgers, potato chips, old money, new—
gay men gather at High Tension
for the annual barbecue
and I, grillmeister,
attend the flame of three grills;
two for the meat, one for the buns.
The best thing to do
is observe the ritual gathering of friends
pronounce it good and get paid.
Campari on ice
tastes good in the shade.
After beef mixed with capers
and spice (slapped into balls not patties)
after seconds & thirds—
out comes red, white and blue:
strawberries over vanilla ice cream
with blueberries from Maine.
This is the fullness
of biblical kings
but not the end of our reign.
The rest of the afternoon is free, let it ring.

EXECUTIVE ON A SUNNY AFTERNOON

Yes it is summer, a wave falls,
bird song rises to open windows,
grass grows in humid breeze,
lawn music echoes in the trees.

Soft, somehow low, a long, slow
yearning for water drowns
out afternoon clatter of computer
and the phone, no one is alone.

For those who meet in rooms
do what it is they have to do,
pretend to perform once again
a repetition gone sour with mold.

To leave work early, beat traffic
home and dream of oxygen
is normal, but we can't leave
until you finish the dull report.

ART FAIR

Arm in arm they tour the gallery rows
she in dress and heels, many rings,
he a fedora, bow tie, jacket,
leather gloves (Summer of Glove)
stroll and chat
the absurdity of art and fashion
moon's connection to our passion
proximity of Champagne
diabolical nature of the market—
lovers high on living well
do not think that thou shall not kill
applies to corporations
so would rather have it now than not.

BIRD LADY

Even from the road they recognize
her face and fly to a beach
she frequents
with a rucksack of hard boiled
eggs or fish parts
from local fishermen.
One by one
she feeds the gulls—
some approach, some refrain
as if to say I'm not hungry today.
A special bird
perches in her nest of hair,
eats hand to beak.
They flap and scream
for food
until the bag is gone.
She rubs sand between her hands
and lights a cigarette,
smoke ascends.
Topless, in a thong, tan
the bird lady scans
the bay for signs, appreciates
time balanced on a leg.
She rises
to walk in the water and swim
out of sight, gulls leap
with animal eyes
to track their provider from above.

TRESPASSES

We plan to hike through various estates in moonlight,
post-derby stomp to celebrate winning horses
but choose another bottle of rosé
and dozen oysters on ice, silver platter
molten in hotel lamplight—

then a dumpster romance,
Pakistani on the Mercedes, thick black curls,
cops in shutdown towns at midnight, rain boots
dance to accelerated crescendos of bass,
Ecuadorian neighbors wake and the journey resumes.

THE CONCERT

In the beginning there was dance
outside the lodge and peace
before the passion.
Rain clouds
sun and stars came out.
The deck was wet.
An argument with a bouncer
got Ben kicked out.
The entreaty
on the ride home
do anything you want to me.
Guests walk,
our bones become clouds
love is lightning
we have
deep sensors
dry grass ignites.
Watching for a candle
waiting for a flood
we yearn for friction to dance.

EAST LANDING

Midnight stumbles down to the bay
to smoke a bowl and pluck a stone
from pebbly shore, fling it sideways,
each skip sparked, each spot rock
connects with knocks day into night
and echoes—miracles await friction.

Skin against the black purse of water
makes a million lights appear,
the shimmering illusions, jellyfish,
put a heavy heart back at ease,
burdens break apart like fireworks
reflected on the rippled surface.

The best place to watch an orgasm
of bright color paint the soaring sky
with beautiful views, all singular
in their floral patterns, joy bombs;
anchored sailboats sitting open—
mouthed as the universe looks on.

Above all the shining stars are loud
and higher than us, our vantage,
this empty lot, will birth a mansion
for others to see abundant planets
and trace reckless laughter on shore,
but for now, us locals own the view.

DRUM CIRCLE

Moon over sea, one lover under
another, the tribal call,
salad and sangria,
dance on sand
connected by starlight
hand in hand we walk away
from ghost rhythms
pulsing ocean,
feet stomp and hips gyrate
waves beat the shore,
swim out too far
and sleep under sand,
sometimes the sky bleeds
and sun drowns,
leaving us to hike desert dunes.

CLAMMING; FOR ANNINA

You ask what it's like and I always
　　　favor commissions, especially
against war and for money
　　　but literary agent, can you
tolerate vulgarity—
　　　it's rather dirty to grasp
all these *Mercenaria mercenaria*.

First remove your clothes or wear
　　　something light and loose
to allow legs to move
　　　and feeling from toe to torso,
then bend in muck
　　　and position your body
over the hole where they hide.

Fingers go in figure eight shapes,
　　　subtle pulse of the earth,
dig for the prize,
　　　sea made love to land
giving birth to buried eggs,
　　　pale portion of shellfish
in the brown, aromatic harbor bed.

>——>

It makes me insane like a gambler
    won't stop trying to win,
who follows intuition
    and thrusts in darkness
for a rush of success in hand,
    for the moment one
with mysterious things in nature.

Luck or skill, look for an opening,
    reach for all or nothing
matters, play the game, hold
    onto your bucket,
savory lumps of luscious meat
    are down there for you
literary agent, whenever you wish.

PROMENADE

It's bliss to walk another man's sweetheart
before an idle crowd, picnics spread
blankets in the grass,
vehicles reversed to a white line
for animals of life to meet civil guests,
a lady wears her dress like it is love,
a man's jacket is a shield
from hardship and vice, kids sell seashells
painted with rainbow stars—
hats off the national anthem,
palm to chest, a young soprano sings,
we slip behind horse trailers
but she protests, would rather go
down stony paths to a top secret lake
through trees and emerge
to prehistoric birds flying funerals
in the sky, then swim naked in sepia water.

St. Michael holds a staff to the face
    of a demon on the ground,
It's body humanesque, twists round
    the feet of his wry figure.

Knight of the Lord, kingdom of man,
    who can possibly guess
What it is they do not understand,
    who remember statues

While the horses sprint on lawns
    lined with fantastic tents,
General admission seats opposite
    VIP lounges for the rich?

Champagne, grapes, crackers, cheese
    on blankets in light dress
And our Michael, a patriarch here,
    designer of French gardens,

Surveys a coterie of event sponsors
    with soft chairs and coolers
Full of what is no doubt delicious,
    lifts his voice in Irish glee.

"Come then, let's replace the divots,"
  as the last few players trot
To the stables, we mount our legs
  and weave unto this ritual:

Gobs of people stroll the fine green
  to flip with toe and stomp
Mounds of sod back in place, mallet
  and hoof strike at a ball,

Bamboo shafts swing from horses
  speeding in slow motion,
They quickly cover the long field
  and thunder the earth

While we cheer the ablest riders
  to keep a tenacious pace—
Though men on horses dig up clods
  the goal is to be great.

Our match ends before we know it
  the award ceremony begins,
Michael rummages in ice and grins
  "come then, another bottle."

BENEFIT CRASHERS

How coincidental we arrive just
in time for fireworks, or do spirits fly
us to luxuriate on a lawn—
bottles at a mansion plus ones
the anonymity of guests
gazing on a harbor
battery of boats
below lights exploding
from their center
percussive blast, report
and echo in brittle darkness
children scurry back to their parents,
boldness rewarded, life accepts us.

WHAT THE SPIRIT

I trespass deep in the Pollack Estate
because the marsh is fecund,
though it sounds dirty
that's how it is. Enormous
maples guard the house
but we don't talk
about how the dead live
or mist in the air,
memory is a fine dust over all.

Look for signs, certain indications,
wisteria hangs from the trees,
stretching in sunlight
I read your poem
and ache, what might have been,
everything
outside your window.
As light, invisible grains
blast the air we inhale the fever.

She spoke the word, the name, the symbol and knew
    the bitter joy it brought,
She was one who unknowingly represents
Another yet outshines the original,
Her voice more powerful, her person undeniable.

Mother called her daughter, love her husband
    yet she did not listen,
Her eyes were fastened to mine
And we were one, total strangers to each other,
A woman on the shore and I, unacquainted,
Joined in a mysterious agreement.

Come on said her daughter, let's go her husband
    yet she did not move,
Just stood and stared in my eyes.

Again the word, the name, the symbol she saw
    written on my soul,
Then spoke in a sympathetic whisper.

She stood still as her family called
    and stopped to watch,
Wondered what happened, what would happen.

My eyes begged her to leave,
Thanked her, gasped as she turned
And shuddered as the waves crashed in my ears.

ANNIVERSARY

Who knows what will happen
start in the kitchen—
fresh clams, fennel, squash
on wood table
herb turns the feast a dance
singers raise their voices
instruments appear
on a deck
we watch the moon
and stars respire,
more wine,
let's rename constellations
as tree leaves twist
their stems in shadow,
spine to asphalt
I search the night with you.

AT NIGHT THEY PLAY

Long hours of work are hard for sure
weigh heavy on skin and bone,
when human grace cannot endure
the burden gets overthrown.

Here gather women, children, men and pets
to enjoy recreation's calm effect,
because our population grows with stress
all crowd the park for leisure, nature soothes
and games of ease relax exhausted folk—
the working class depends upon its back
yet somehow manages to find the strength
to go on, to stand up and demonstrate.

Easy weather, do not rain this evening,
sports are scheduled, people count on inning,
half and match to rouse their weary spirits
to athletic feats and revive from
daily struggle with miraculous pitch,
kick and swing before their family
or casual spectators, have mercy,
let no storm delay a communal gathering.

Fun calls the cult of exercise to feed,
to head outside and run around,
without the freedom of movement
there'd be a riot in every town.

THE OCTET

Moment when music performs a miracle
interwoven with strings,
a childhood memory, a future dream.
The old church is a spaceship
of colonial architecture.
Friends with kids
across the country, infinite feelings
in the palm of a hand.
Words released from captivity
blue curtains painted on the wall,
a profile in the balcony.
Once there was jazz
you could see all the way up the steeple.

MENDELSSOHN

I wrote in your hand
the unspeakable
music
forms a net
around us.
You are the sun
of summers
to come.
Every memory
starts again
wherever you go
look into your hand.

In an epoch ripe for ceremony
    thirsty adults gather to taste
various wines at vineyards
    ideal for literary readings.

With nose and tongue select
    diverse distillations of grape
for subtle flavor and bouquet,
    perhaps to string quartets.

They lounge on sunlit patio
    with bottles of chilled white,
some sweet, others dry, and
    chat with old acquaintance.

Then soft cheese and cherries,
    rosemary-encrusted bread,
almonds, avocado, chocolates
    followed by chicory coffee.

After naps ride to The Sound
     to watch the water heave
or take gentle strokes offshore,
     casually surface to breathe.

It is a treat to live out east
     on heaven's isle, tomorrow
comes quite regularly, time
     passes within an eye's blink.

FOR ESTELLA

Blessed to record existence
the seasons cannot steal
I have inspiration—
day and night
are bliss
sweat and salt
on suntanned skin
the hour lifts
a round and luscious
flame of consummation
a kiss tops
each reason the ocean
swallows every sin.

WINE GODDESS

The acme of summer fills baskets
with fresh fruit and vegetables
at country stands; each morning
a corpse appears on city streets
that reek of sweat and decay.

Invitations to feast fill my calendar
with wild flowers: vast chicory,
bee balm, yarrow, composite daisy
adorn roadsides that border
a hundred kinds of delicious crops.

May words always carry pictures:
black curly hair, white cotton dress,
without knowing it this season
turns a bitter festival in haste—
why be tearful, why not celebrate?

CONFESSION

Pounds and pounds the water
with rage returned tears
to the sea,
facing things, say goodbye
to the one you wish
could stay.
Cigarette smoke drifts
from the pier.
Remember cello and violin
cast a net-like spell
from finger
to palm blind message.
Remember the words we said.

There's a murder of crows in my yard,
A lawnmower polluting the environment,
The rotted leftovers of a hundred refrigerators
    thrown out for compost,
A migrant worker taking a shortcut—
Squirrels are the main attraction.

Perhaps this is their local insane asylum
    but I've observed others
In different towns, in the country
And not found stable squirrels,
On the contrary, studies prove they
    are mentally abnormal,
Rodents who revel in perilous situations.

They sprint the length of tree limbs and leap
Without hesitation to no specific place,
Grasp whichever branch comes
    to their paws,
Swing like monkeys, twitter, cluck, bark
And can even crow like a rooster.

>—>

They act nervous then dart behind trees,
Are unpredictable, seem paranoid,
　　have busy imaginations,
Indifferent acrobats on telephone poles,
　　lovers of power lines stunts.

Watching them play, I note excitability
　　during social interactions,
A compulsion to give chase for sport
　　or territorial aggression,
Either way, unforgettable displays;
Wrestling, boxing and tackling each other.

Why are the critters so frantic?
It's known squirrels like shelled meat,
　　which may explain things,
When not with mates they constantly seek it,
That it's hard to find accounts for their
　　lack of self-control,
Hunger goes straight to their heads,
Squirrels are mad about nuts.

AUGUST

The hydrangeas have bruised,
give way to trumpet vines
and roadside sumacs,
airborne clusters of orange.

HORSE SHOW

It will never happen like this again—
let's have brunch and toast
the passage.
Cocktails taste better
in the morning.
There's no fault free journey.
A horse nears the jump,
hoof clicks rail
and clears.
Some land easy, others hard,
Fabulous leads the way
with Paul O'Shea.
A ringmaster in red livery
raises his post horn
and sounds
the call—the jump off is on.
Skies are clear,
young jumpers clean and fast,
a courteous woman
wipes a bug off my back.
Once Tom
saw a horse flip
backwards and break its rider's arm.

BEAUTIFUL DREAMER

I imagine the weight of your body flies
beyond trees to enter clouds—
connection without name,
scent of grass, music in the wind,
finely threaded sheets,
a symphony from your window,
fallen leaves, crisp and dry
on the street in morning light,
to kiss ethereal lips
and breathe a mortal sigh,
flesh come alive,
the deep blue field you hold inside.

A hand reaching to the sky
revolves in forever,
heaven is your hair pillowed on a bed,
a hill for dreams to launch their winged arms.

THE CHECK

You wonder how a lion gets so loose
each season, hunger licks its lips
without regard for property or price.

Perhaps a minx ignites the flame,
humid eyes project hot
afternoons of leisure in the sun.

And wine, give us our nightly bottles
to sleep and forget, then laugh
at those who bet against us.

Pride is worth the additional expense,
summer ends, tour complete,
someone pay the check, let's leave.

You came from Ecuador
Whether your family was rich or poor, how many
    brothers or sisters you had
Or what your early childhood was like—
I'm sad to say I do not know.

As a young man you got mixed up with cocaine.
Your father kicked you out of your home.
You fathered two kids of your own.

I don't know what happened next
Or how you took care of your new family
    but you left Ecuador
To earn a better living in Chicago
    and sent money home.

In the windy city you witnessed
The magnificent heights and squalid lows
    of a paradox culture,
Working as a busboy and part-time bartender
    in a fancy hotel,
You got married and had another child.

For five years you lived and worked here Diego,
    this country became yours,
Walked along the lake, made new friends,
Saw museums watched skyscrapers
And finally enjoyed life.

I don't know what brought you to the Hamptons,
A more lucrative job or something else?
Whatever led you to these elegant shores,
    to cut down trees,

Pour concrete, rake and remove leaves—
You got a job with a wealthy man
Who offered to sell his truck in exchange
    for time and money.

I met you one morning with hammer in hand,
Sunny spikes gleamed like silver dollars
We joined in a common struggle
    to dredge a pond
And haul shit with the wheelbarrow.
It was then you told me your story.

>—→

You spoke of plans for the future—
To save money, buy a house, get married
    and have another child,
To continue sending monthly payments
    to Chicago and Ecuador.

With a girlfriend in Queens
Who wanted to see you every night,
You borrowed the truck before the deal was done.

I don't know why you got drunk or arrested
Or were in jail for an entire month
    which seems excessive,
Diego Rivera, I was grateful for your company,
    for making the day better,
For laughter where there was none before.

AFTER LABOR DAY

When vacation finishes
lovers leave town.
Water is cold
at swimming season's close.
Back to the office,
walks home in the rain
tree silhouettes
and I see your face
in the outline of a mud puddle,
delicately contoured.
Art gone, deer roam the roads.

OCCASIONS

It is not just the end of summer's
intoxication in villages
with new friends,
on cliffs overlooking Portugal
waves submerse rocks
for a moment
rocks reappear,
unmoved by tidal change
mud on the path
a treasure,
gala tents come down
on Sunday
the expressway calls
the city calls,
we hike trails above the ocean,
share donuts and beer
as the sun sets
and full moon rises
in unison, their polar energy
bisects the earth—
our hands connect the dots again.

THE MURDER

They call and call
in otherworldly words.

Turned from a nightmare
I look out the window
at beak and eye and claw
feathers midnight blue
all that's lost remains.

Prophetic from the gutter
presence sure as mine
fly to the treetop
and pilfer summer's best—
dropped to the yard
it fits a hollow in my chest.

NOTHING IS MEANINGFUL

Summer swims in a sea of seasons,
crawling through water to eye the sky,
sunbathers mark surface reflections,
blood-red ribbons of deeper light
darken the horizon.

    Why is it we
who live with death, watch the sun slip
into casual nothing for an hour,
set the dinner table and sail away
with a sip of Cognac in Champagne?

WHAT THE SEA STOLE

Hold tide, hold your copious motion a minute
While I replay a summer tragedy for
All to seize the danger inherent—
Days begin alike until something changes.

Families gather for weekend picnics on the beach,
    friends sunbathe and swim,
Wind picks up and settles down children
    run rampant on the sand,
People party their days off,
Water makes life bearable for local and tourist
Where land leaves them disappointed.

It is freedom they seek, those surfers who brave
    sharks and squalls to ride,
Who mount the equine wavery, harness wild
    fluid power on boards
And heel the breaking thrust of gravity.

Others enjoy calm walks on sunlit shores,
    a gilded ocean surface
And soak in leisure, entranced by gulls
That float above the human crowd,
    dive down for handouts
Or invade blankets, screaming with laughter.

❯⟶

Couples lay quietly or talk of serenity,
Others play volleyball, radios echo off umbrellas,
    the salty odor pervades
As several people stare at the bright water
    with curious faces,
Shielding their eyes with their hands.

Someone calls to two young boys gone too far
    from shore, they are brothers
And best friends, more, they drift apart.

The louder, more urgent, second call,
A lone surfer grabs his board, sprints to the water
    and swims as fast as he can.

The third call is a cry for help.
Only one conversation occurs, some hold phones
    others wade into the turbulence.

A rip tide carries the brothers out to sea
And tears them apart, one floats further away.

➤⟶

The fourth call determines boats and helicopters
    are on their way,
The lone surfer reaches the nearest boy
But cannot see the other, only hears a shout
    "where is my brother?"

Life is in peril as the surfer swims
Back to shore with what little strength he has left,
And the boy he has saved cries aloud.

Grown men and women, fathers and mothers
    themselves, openly weep,
They've experienced loss but this is worse.
When the surfer returns with the boy
    none can silence,
Not now nor ever, to the wave-broken beach,
He just screams "my brother is dead!"

It's true, humor cannot change it,
That two young boys once went for a swim
And even after extensive search, only one survived.

TO THE PUBLISHER

This is the effect, winged repercussion,
  feathers spread across the sky,
echo over an empty parking lot
  and they're off, leaves from trees.

BLOOD BROTHERS

Remember when we went down to the river
to drink big cans of beer in paper sacks
and throw rocks at rats
that crept from the banks
like ground shadows?
It's dusk; wind
and tall grass on my knees
the sun sets over Accabonac Harbor.
The tide is at its lowest point.
I wade in the water
with a child's pail to dig for clams
with my bare hands
their hard shell
a perfect fit for a palm,
standing in the slimy seaweed
I reckon not even death can separate us.

THE DEAL

I know you when the kitchen chair
creaks with a weight that is not there.
You fly the earth and see the sun
as I honor the deal to watch
a girl become a woman.

Give us night to sleep and forget
all of life is impermanent.
The wine gets put away, the shade
comes down, the candle dances
with a shadow it has made.

BEACHED WHALE

It lay there vacant-eyed,
Sixty-six feet of mammalian demigod for all to ogle,
    spouting saline geysers no more,
Tongue protruding out enormous slack jaw,
A once colossal grace gone motionless.

The large crowd gathers round its alien cadaver
    with cameras silent, eager
To take it all in, but unsure exactly how,
None have seen a bigger beast in suit of flesh.

Hesitant to arrive at partial conclusion,
Apt to want the full story, people curiously circle
Unable to resist an enormous speculation.

For it lay on the grand scale where
Myth grows realistic and divinity dissolves,
The single being that outweighs others deceased.

A LEAF

Broken stem, cracked edges,
all that is the leaf
flakes to dust—
ghost feet
put whole trees under.
A leaf is a tear
that falls
with infinite others.
Everything
is silent
as it touches the ground.

BY THE ROAD

I.

When all songs come back
at once, echo on a barge, music
and storm rock unusual instruments,
water is a slow horse, city gleams—
    time to start over.

    I offer moments
apart from everything, a September
stroll after the show (who are we
when we are together?) to a café
about to close, and discuss it further.

You are dead or something
unlike seduction. One plays the role
of sexual redeemer, another
sacrifices love on a watery alter.
It's not passion but possibility.
I would rather leap a fence
    and dive in darkness.

After dinner? Having been impaled
　　the thing to do is escape,
that's why cars exist, so goodbye
　　critic of the bloody organ.

　　The night is new
and different souls await (but
who are we now and who
were we then?) city gleams—
　　busy streets, beds
are warm and full of lovers.

　　Beyond the familiar
lies what may be phenomenal,
　　a voice sounds
come to where the leaves
are bright, fresh air
floats over fields,
harvest time is here.

➤—→

II.

Taking a train is a joyous thing
one feels electricity
pulse the rail
tree lines rise and fall
waterways flash
backyard lots
quickly pass
the sun, radiant and new,
laser what's left
of cauliflower, stalk and vine.

We ride forever unconcerned
yet eventually reach
the shore, crawl
through pendulous tide,
strong are waves
that break
inside momentous pause,
swim in deep reunion,
years overlap years,
feel the pull
yet resist it
with embryonic pride.

➤⟶

Back on land for coffee,
a skirt full of thighs
is a postmodern spell
on the yard sale;
desk, jewelry, paintings
rest on shaded lawn,
a gallery in Amagansett;

Chinese espadrille, custom dresses
float the female form
and slip off easily,
driftwood cufflinks, photos
distorted like dreams, smashed
soda cans painted white,
red wine, pistachio, mineral water,
books stacked to the ceiling—
Jesse Elliott design.

Then we leave in a wagon
to cruise through vegetable fields,
sun in full dalliance,
backseat blisses
wind on skin
all aboard
the ferry to Shelter Island.

➤⟶

With land in sight,
country scents
waft between us
a certain look
lingers, hand brushes hand
that does not pull away
the ferry slams
tires bolted to wood pilings.

Chain released,
the metal gate
opens to a boutique
on Sunset Beach.
Nothing matters but the view
to people sipping, people lunching
at their lovely leisure—
our driver honks
time to visit another gallery
in a pew-gutted church

where neo-classic
portraits are self-conscious
outside the window
another gallery
serves malt liquor tall boys
in monogrammed paper bags.

➤—→

How quaint, how Detroit,
hands in the cooler,
mythical beings
half-animal and half-human
conduct a ceremony
in real forest—
we laugh and drink like pagans!

Let's go to dinner, see fireworks,
to temple for string quartet,
waves pound glass
scramble in various cars
to new places,
a full moon
let's meet up later.
The crowd opens
to a bench with extra seats,
slow, sliding violin bow
and cellos whisper.

Beauty and pain
cannot be
adequately expressed.
I miss you but do not linger.

$\longrightarrow$

III.

She enters temple in a vanilla
cashmere gown belted
with tan calfskin,
hair coiffed
brown eyes stars.
She crosses the room
then her legs.
I wear
a navy pinstriped suit,
bombs explode
wood walls shudder
overpowering adagios
the recital ends
applause down hall
let's get in line
for ice cream in East Hampton.

Night has many flavors and
I'm mad to fall in love
with wine, to take
your hand
and flee the lonely hours,
launch our hearts.

➤⟶

IV.

We do everything
bodies circulate at night;
play poker on a patio,
start a bonfire,
dance to electric beats,
have a nightcap at the tavern.

We can say hello
to someone about to die
and not know it
then drive to a house
where nothing happens,
couch in a dark room,
I cover you with my jacket.

OCTOBER

When mums and Montauk
daisies are all that's left;
the gold splendor
of trees with crests aflame.

POEM FOR HILLARY

So what's your destiny she said
I've thought about it
ever since. There's a storm.
Traffic stops
a tree hangs on a power line
over the road ready
to snap a few final yards
to wet pavement. What next?
It was the last time
we ever spoke.
Love is my destiny I said.
She smiled
and unpacked cardboard
boxes loaded with donations.

AN ALLEY DARK

Silver lines split the night
then landed in rough puddle,
wet universe, brown consolation,
music floods abandoned places.

Black bushes lurk at shadow's edge,
lost branches dip within a bleak
entablature of sky, it violates,
something shakes and falls away.

A bell rings not too far out to sea,
minds take brilliant lapses
to be free from all the doubts
that life is real and we are ghosts.

Alone inside yet not without
brick buildings mortared round,
free standing basin, future
reverberations echo loud the storm.

A bird can plash its wings in water
then emerge prepared to fly,
so we can rise from shallow gutter
to beat the air with new life.

VISITATION

Pages stir
I heard a voice
cold wind in trees
candlelight
ancient things
and stars
wishing on hours
the muse
rested a hand
on my shoulder.

THE INNOCENT

To love and lose is hard to do.
Why are days taken away
by misfortune? Stop the clock
that clicks above the door, what's left
but darkness from before? No hand
can bare the morning light.
Who sees the sun? Who knows a thing?
Blinded by nights without end
what can be captured, what defended?
To think another thought—
yet brave souls must brave it again.
It's better not to be born at all.

IN THE WRECKAGE

We are all faces in the sand,
my manifestation
came to tell you
all is lost before the end.

Morbid yet you see
a ship of fate run aground,
executioner toss heads
with industrial precision.

It's not our decision
what becomes of this shore,
you think water accounts
for houses and towns?

Mindless mind moves the sea
whether to flood or flame,
many say the day
of collapse must be so.

Yet the jury is silent
about how things will go,
and I don't pretend to know
what water has in store.

That it can express such sadness
in the early morning is true,
too tough a proposition
to stay solemn—
leaden atmosphere,
daystar statue,
orb steeped in gloomy mist,
moon a bony sliver,
satellite obscure,
evening sinks a battered ship—
seabird soliloquy, rebel
in the night alone it cries for you.

TOTAL ECLIPSE

I looked at the poem
and knew it was
possible to take
back roads
to the highway,
that soon
we would swim
in the ocean again.
Poems are born
of eye connections,
not torn out
to appall jailors,
but sewn
with the rhythm
of breath.
Words mean
nothing like stars,
the total eclipse
on a long drive home.

GULLS

The sea steals in the sea
buries tide on land
hammers horse hooves
ashore, wind
blasts glassy sand.
The surface is uneasy,
light on water
I cannot continue
gulls swoop like ghosts.

Cheers for love, athletic season, love once felt
    forevermore and left
A lone fountain to scale the deluge rain,
Uplifts and elevates meridian,
Single jet against the rest, memory made.

Still the candle rises
Amid talk at tables set for reception,
Couples stand outside museum and hall
With dinner plans in stylish dress,
Evening crowds gather to salute the sunset
    with glasses full of joy.

A toast to absent guests, celebrated friends,
They may have climbed stairs and leapt
    off laughter's rooftop,
Their existence may be conjecture
However, we scan identical sets of stars.

Abstracts of summer,
Seawater splashes the air unattached,
Lit mist saturates our vision with excess,
The reason is obscure—wounded,
    something arrives
To stretch a second into an eternity of flight.

CLIFF WALK

Take precipice removed from slapping waves
of sharp erosion, where excitements keep
and people strip to jump in the sea,
where misty mansions line a pristine shore.

I think about life and dive to meet you
on the dark floor, that place where death does
not matter, then rise, fists full of sand
and breathe with wings, lungs transformed.

Far more than walls of stone can demarcate
or effervescence thrill, flight and descent,
water is our favorite place to play—
take orgasmic leaps off everything concrete.

THE KAYAKER

Dressed as a slippery seal
he steps in frigid sea
to wade through
overturning
basins of lawless wave,
rides down
watery slopes,
buoyed or bulldozed
by the surf
the sea rolling
as it rolled ages ago,
churns foam,
he revolves and thrashes
left then right
caught in the turbine,
fishtails sideways and jets.

ADIEU DEERFIELD

We are our best in congregation,
the well-set marble table
piano key painting
black and blue enharmonics
Buddha under an orchid
fake Jeff Koons,
geese shit on the patio,
Larry sells bricks
for seventy-five bucks
to a loud man from Springs.
There's a frame
around the fireplace
low seated couch and chairs
tie-died pillows
let's leave the upstairs
for imagination.
We ate sweet corn
leftover grilled chicken
Waldorf Salad
and peach pie for desert.

The piano
key painting
shifts your focus
from negative to positive.
Mark does not title
his pieces or
sign them on the front.
We aren't in Watermill anymore.

ANATOMY OF A WAVE

The flight of geese across expansive territory,
clouds part, intermittent honks become
an occasion to pause from work,
the formation hardly a V
rather broken imitations of it
yet they weave their way
through taller space
than other birds
and I grow
wings of love because the earth
passes below as I fly above
the produce fields and water spread
to embrace what is no more.

TREES AND THEIR NUTS

You have a way of letting go
things you do not need.
Trees fling
their nuts
to the ground.
I gravitate to you
my heart
is full of seed
the wind says let go.

EAST OF AMAGANSETT

What a shock to find the person
  you would most like to meet
holding a glass of wine at a party
  for a holy festival by the sea.

Such people haunt post offices
  with large eyes and cell phones,
Speak like multiethnic travelers
  in rural, homogenous zones

And take photographs to design
  things that address the era.
They drink bitter indigenous tea
  with lemon and agave nectar,

Smoke herb with glee and dance
  to electro-hop sans shame.
I met one who was like a dream
  and became the harbinger

For new love, when split logs fell
  from axe to driveway, it was
Time to run around the house
  and thank stars above the ocean.

PECONIC BAY

If life should fail to be on good ground
let it return to the grand Peconic,
rest one knee in water, one on land,
conjoin a salty accession of swells
to swollen eyes and lips, kiss the calm,
otherworldly wet, power unseen.

Sorrow overruled, mortal mania
no longer lingers like mean perfume,
the broken body redeemed
on dappled shore, transparent bay,
wind careens into steep bluffs
and sends sand avalanches to the beach.

GHOSTS

Houses and cars are full of illusions,
the presence or absence of property is minor—
we are ghosts in this ghost world
what counts are correlations.

Acknowledgements:

Tom Arnott, N. Thane Boulton, Arlene Bujese, Siv Cedering and
Hans Van de Bovenkamp, Ben Cawiezell, Jesse Elliott, Sarah Gerard,
Renita Guyanand, Jack W.C. Hagstrom, Mary Hevy, Carol Hunt,
Marilyn and Thomas Hunt, Mark Humphrey & Larry Rundie,
Teri Kennedy, Gina and Peter Koper, Theresa Murphy, The Lights,
Valerie and Chad McCarthy, Kate and Jim McMullan, Jeffrey Nolte,
Lukas Ortiz, Murat Oztaskin, Kathryn Solow, Mary & Philip Spitzer,
and Regiane Queiroz.

Thank you dearly Madeleine, Christina Daigneault & Simon Van Booy.

CPSIA information can be obtained
at www.ICGtesting.com
Printed in the USA
BVHW071923220519
548968BV00002B/5/P